Entremaneur

Entremaneur

Business Solutionists!

Mitch Ellner

To order additional copies of this book, contact:
Xlibris Corporation
1-888-795-4274
www.Xlibris.com
Orders@Xlibris.com
48158

Contents

The Other "—maneur"

Appendix

Introduction

Foreword

Why This Book?

This book should be considered a serious account about business with an emphasis on how to have fun in business, and how having fun and getting the job done gets muddy in the complexity we create. We have an obsession with complicating the most traditional and simplistic aspects of what we do every day—communicate and perceive. This book is a work in progress. Change, then again, isn't business. The one thing you can count on is change? The concept and the theories are just that, are they steadfast rules on how to conduct ourselves in business, are they the only way to do things, are they the "medicine" for curing everything that is an opportunity and/or is an alignment of our businesses? NO! The answers you know and we will continue to assess throughout this process. They are truly snapshots of your business, which takes the most simple and most complex aspects and puts them together in a process of simplicity—like a reel of film playing a story!

The concept is based upon reality—yet what a concept. They are intended to be simple, with lots of visualization and explanations that are easy to understand and follow. It is about knowing the difference and when to make changes even if it is not your outlined way of doing business. It is understanding that everything we do is based upon people, communication, interaction, interpretation, and perception. And it is about all of us—YOU!

When this project began, you can imagine the amount of creative feedback I received from friends, family, and colleagues. The title itself conjures more analogies than one can or should choose to handle, and, of course, it more appropriately brought out the comedian in everyone (or so they thought—NOT).

The goal is to bring a smile to your face, provide a realistic view at business in an effort to instill a simplistic approach to accomplishing the goals, measuring, monitoring, and adjusting accordingly. Learn it! Use it! Make it a reality!

There are many a skeptic and many a person that will say there is another way, a better way, a more extensive way, a more expensive way, a way to keep the consultants running the business, etc., etc., etc. Without a doubt, there is more than one way to process and do "snapshots" of the business; yet this process is defined as simple, useful, and transferable immediately into your business. These are the keys to the concept. Are there other ways to do it, look at it, etc.? You bet, and they may produce similar results. So all we can say is that you be the judge and see how simple it is and how transferable it is, as the process is YOUR "snapshots" to YOUR business and easily adjusted to modify, change, and/or project YOUR business.

Enjoy the process, as it is fun and, most importantly, realistic. I hope you have as much fun reading and implementing as I did developing and writing it!

"Manure" to "Maneur"—without a doubt this is a play on words, yet can you think of any better play? Do you feel as if you are in a pasture with land mines of manure constantly? Well hopefully, what this will do for you is assist in sidestepping manure to walking the line of maneur—cultivating and moving forward!

The process is industry agnostic. All businesses have the same elements as identified below—simple! If you do not have a plan, then there is truly no action—simple! It then ='s "manure" instead of "maneur"—confusion, lack of clarity, rework, $'s, etc.

Entremaneur = Finance (Results) + Operations (Metrics)
+ Performance (Human Capital)

So sit back and relax. Grab a bag of popcorn, and just like the movies, only "reel" (you'll see) watch the story of YOUR business unfold!

How the Book Reads

Each chapter of the book is designed to follow the concept of entremaneur, and that is simple! Therefore, the following premise has been established for the book and sections so that it is simple and consistent.

What Is It (Vision)?

This defines what it is that is being done and what it is all about. It further defines the introduction and/or explanation to the concept/section. Much like the vision, it is about a quick yet clear and concise statement on what this all about or what you see. Again taking the concept of snapshots, what is the image you want to project outward and then point, click, and there is the what!

How Does It Work? What Will It Do for Me/Us (Strategies)?

This part of the process is where the rubber hits the road or, in "snapshot" terms, where the film is developed into an actual picture. Think of digital photography, where you take the picture, see the image, and decide if it is what you want or retake or even touch up. This is what the how is. How do I simply take what is being done and implement it into my/our world and reality and not just have a bunch of theoretical jargon and concepts that in "theory" make sense, yet in reality, "What and how the heck do I translate this into my world—simply, consistently and regularly?" In other words, how do I use it and not let it be like other things and grow dust on a shelf, so to speak?

What Are the Actions and/or Costs (Activities)?

Once you have taken the picture and seen how it will work, now is the time to define the picture into a realistic implementation and generate interest and use. When thinking of YOUR business, it is about how the minimal concepts will be used; and the key here is setting actions that they will be used, because the entire concept of entremaneur is about daily practical and useful applications! The actions become the activities that are done to perform the strategies, and the strategies are formed from the how. So in simplest terms, what is vision, how is strategies and actions are activities simple and concise! In every business, the costs will vary. Here you see them up front and in real time, so understanding and adjusting becomes simple. YOUR business costs will be defined as you entremaneur your business.

Welcome to Entremaneur!

Let's talk entremaneur—what is it, what and how will I use it, and what are the actions?

Like doctors, Entremaneur is a diagnostic review of your business, a recommendation for treatment, a prescription of how to do it yourself, follow up, measurement and management of the entire process.

Chapter 1

What is Entremaneur?

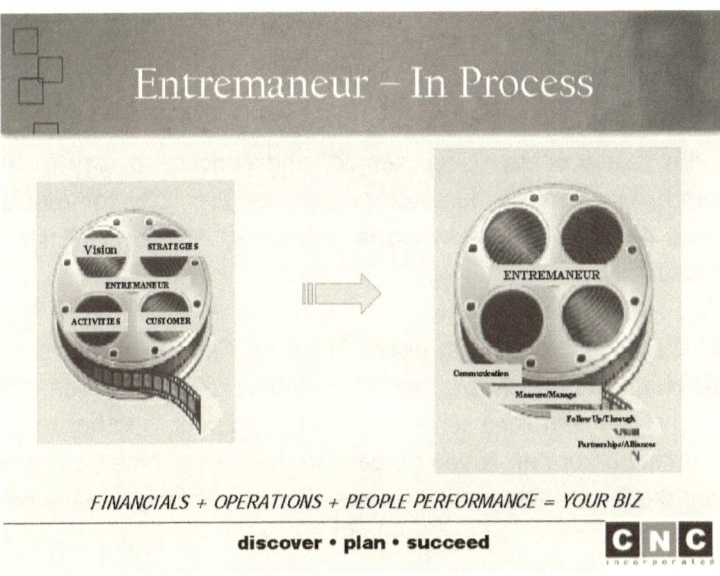

FINANCIALS + OPERATIONS + PEOPLE PERFORMANCE = YOUR BIZ

discover • plan • succeed

Step 1 - Preliminary Business Strategy Solution *Profile*

- Individual
- Group Comparison

Step 2 – Entremaneur Strategic Solution *Process*

- Organization Chart
- People & Time Chart
- Dollar Allocation Chart
- Vision, Strategy and Activity alignment Chart

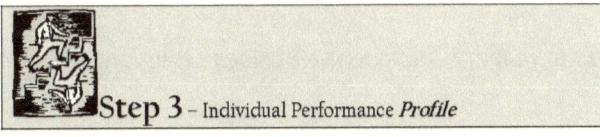

Step 3 – Individual Performance *Profile*

- Activity Performance Alignment Profile – Performance Management

What Is Entremaneur?

Finances + Operations + People Performance = Your Business

What is it?

Entremaneur is a process—clear, simple, and concise—a way to measure, monitor, and manage your business and create simplicity for real time use of **Finances *(results)* + Operations *(metrics)* + People Performance *(human capital)*!**

Confused? Well, join the business world! The term, like any others, can be used in many fashions and transforms itself many a time to fit a situation. The reality is that anyone can coin themselves as an entrepreneur whether they truly fit the entire definition or not. If you go back to developing times, the word *entre* comes from the French and means "between and/or among." The word *maneur* can have multiple meanings; yet coming from the derivative, it truly means to cultivate. So with that said, then *entre* and *maneur* mean the following:

"Entre" defined means—Entre is used as the entrance or entrée to the process, or in its literal translation from the old-time French, it is between or amongst, which in business translation pertains to between or amongst business situations, dealings, or producing such things as to be bring together for business fundamentals.

"Maneur" defined is—Maneur is an actual play on the word *manure* as the most realistic business situation are always sidestepping the potential land mines of manure instead of simply managing the business and the direct communications associated as such. Coming from the French word *entrepreneur* or *entrepreneurship*, which is defined above, the actual word *maneur* is derived from the word *manouver* meaning "to cultivate."

"Entremaneur" defined is—Business solutionists!

How Does It Work? What Will It Do for Me/Us (Strategies)?

Entremaneur is a process. What the process does is combine the finances, operations, and people performance into a snapshot that is a usable and workable solution to managing the current business, identifying projections and planning. The entremaneur process does not replace strategic business plans, financial plans, and/or performance management, yet combines all three in a simplistic format to measure and manage your business. This process can be the pre and/or post to any business planning.

So for our purposes, entremaneur is the process of bringing together the business and cultivating it in a simplistic and efficient fashion to deliver snapshots based upon Financials *(Results)* + Operations + *(Metrics)* + People Performance (Human Capital) = YOUR Business *(Entremaneur)*. Continuing with my warped interpretation of it—reminding me of and being similar to the Wizard of Oz—entremaneur to Dorothy and the gang is defining a game plan to get through the forest (strategy), delegating out the tasks (activities) and getting to the Emerald City to get home (vision).

Long about the time businesses got underway is about the time that we as business professionals began complicating the very essence of every aspect of what we do. We began miscommunicating, not saying what we mean, not setting clear expectations, not providing needed information when necessary, sabotaging our coworkers to get ahead, not asking questions, not creating a vision to have a clear direction, not tying or not creating strategies yearly to achieve the vision, and, lastly, not tying performance of the company, the people, and the results to the strategies, which ties to the vision, which connects the knee bone to the hip bone—see how complex it gets?

Well long about the time we have spent centuries messing all this up, we still have not realized that we have made it more complicated and complex; so we add more processes, with more forms, and before you know it we are not using the old stuff anymore, useful or not. Yet we have moved on to a whole new set of confusing and useless, nontied-to-results processes.

So since I have now thoroughly got you spinning with more complexity and confusion, I should end this book here and leave it like it has been for generations and centuries and eras, etc.—confused, muffled, and thoroughly confusing. Now do you really think I would do that to you? Plus, my therapist would be so disappointed that I did not follow through to completion on one of my set actions.

The basics of entremaneur deal with the most simplistic and yet the most complicated business life process known as communications. Communications in all of its forms—written, verbal, and graphical—can and should define our business processes in a simplistic fashion. What we have done in business is complicate the process to the point of walking through a land mine of manure in a pasture and never quite knowing where to step, what we'll step on, and what the outcome will be. What entremaneur does is take all the years of complications in years of business and simplify into snapshots to manage. Measure and communicate regularly, effectively, and efficiently all the time. Sound easy or complicated? You choose. If you want to stay in the land mines of manure, continue doing what you are doing. If you want to change to a process of simplicity, then entremaneur yourself: Financials + Operations + People Performance = Your Business—your snapshot.

Writing about business and vision, strategy and activities, always makes me think of the almighty Wizard of Oz.

There is always so much action and drama surrounding everything we do in business, much as to Dorothy and her crew finding their way to Oz. Yet once there, it came down to something simple, and *that* we always have known, had we spent a tad bit more time looking, planning, and monitoring. Now do we all have ruby slippers and fairy godmothers? On second thought, don't answer that!

What Are the Actions and/or Costs (Activities)?

The reality is we have the ability to find Oz and find our way home again—simply and efficiently. With a little direction (strategy) and guidance (vision) and a helping teaspoon of follow-through (activities), it is amazing what we can accomplish!

Home is always where it has been; we just need to wade through the pastures of manure to the get to the greener pastures of "maneur."

Making modifications to the information that is inputted and getting new results, projections, anticipations, etc., is what the entremaneur process is about. It is a snapshot of YOUR business as it looks now and how you may want it to look if you make a modification, change, and/or augmentation in any way. The process itself is intuitive and does not need any major programming, consulting time, or the like, yet can be done by the truest of lay person—and trust I am one, so I know from what I speak! You could say it is like installing a simple software package, like your PDA software, phone software, etc.—yet, nah, then I would be lying to you, or at least in my case, I don't think any of them are that simple! Just trust me (I know never trust anyone that says "trust me") that if you keep going down the simple path, the yellow brick road, you will see it really is that simple.

So now talk to me about Finance *(results)* + Operations *(metrics)* + People Performance *(human capital)* = YOUR business. What the heck does that mean? How does it translate into a snapshot of my business? Talk to me. I need to and want to know—NOW!

A True Reality Check

The reality is that most CEOs are busy concentrating on running the business from the perspective of growing sales, improving the operations and the future profitability of the business that they have not and do not take the time to look how they are practicing simple management principles, such as the basics of communication. What ends up getting overlooked is the basic personality traits that each and every one of us brings to the table, and they end up treating all the members of their management team as if they are just like them and have full and total comprehension of everything they say and believe.

Every one of us is a different personality, so is the above possible? NO. The CEO must take the time to explain the vision, strategy, and activities. The *where* the company is now, the *where* it is going, and the *how* he and you plan to get it there. This must be done as a team and individually; otherwise, why would you have these members on your team guiding the vision and strategy of the business, because it becomes like the old game of telephone tag, and by the time the information (vision and strategy) gets through the company, it is completely different. Is this truly an effectively run operation, and is this truly what the CEO has planned for sales, operations, and profitability?

Without this personalization in communications, each manager and employee will have a different "perception" of the vision that the CEO has of the business. Obviously, without this communication, each manager has and operates on a different agenda, and thus alignment, BUSINESS SIMPLICITY—ENTREMANEUR, does not exist. Each member must feel included and that their participation is important and valued to the accomplishment of the vision and strategy, which run the business—bar none! This is the ultimate incentive for anyone.

Entremaneur is the process of this simplicity and quickly gets the team refocused on the CEO's vision and improves the overall communications, which is the most important business function and is, without a doubt, the root of all harmony and dynamics within the operations of YOUR business.

So the question, SIMPLY, is your team in harmony and/or sync with your or the company's vision? If your answer is hesitant or unsure, what are you going to do? Entremaneur YOUR business!

Financials + Operations + Performance = Your Business

So let's get to the simplicity. What are the Financials *(results)*, Operations *(metrics)*, and People performance *(human capital)*?

What Is It (Vision)?

The financials are . . . The financials relate to any and all things dealing with business results. This usually takes the format of a budget template, process, or spreadsheet of some kind, which takes into account all the expense and revenue options, previous statistics if the business has been in operation, and/or projections for current businesses as well as new businesses or entities. The financials in entremaneur are like all other aspects, a snapshot of the business known as the results. This process, which will be defined in greater detail in an upcoming chapter, is the detail and drill down for creating the overall "entremaneur snapshot" of YOUR business.

The operations are . . . The operations deals with setup of the business, the organizational structure, the strategies, the vision, and how all this combined provides the basis for which our businesses are built on, or in most cases should be built on. Now with that said, this does not mean we begin a series of meetings and writing exercises to make pretty statements that float on people's screen savers, are posted in our lobbies and community areas, become mantras for marketing, etc. What it does mean is that we identify these factors as the underlying premise for our business and then use them to produce the activities that each person works toward to meet them and make it simple for them to see how they fit and follow the strategies and vision and for us to measure and manage appropriately. We spend way too much time writing these out and meeting on what they should be, instead of spending the time to make them useful and useable and snapshots of simplicity that all can see and model ourselves and our performance or anticipated or projected performance against. This process, which will be defined in greater detail in an upcoming chapter, is the mantra of vision and strategies in which to meet this vision, which creates the overall "entremaneur snapshot" of YOUR business.

The people performance is . . . Wow, this is where the rubber meets the road or the feet hit the yellow brick road. How complicated have we in business made this process? How have we taken what people do to achieve results and tried to tie to company performance, yet not given the tools on how the company performance is derived, calculated, and how each person individually fits to and aligns to the business strategies and vision, and shown each person how they are only three steps away from the overall vision of the company, the heartbeat of who it is, what it stands for, and how it gets things accomplished—the performance (each individual doing what they do—"activities")? This process, which will be defined in greater detail in an upcoming chapter, is the people performance, detail, and drill down for creating the overall "entremaneur snapshot" of YOUR business.

How Does It Work? What Will It Do for Me/Us (Strategies)?

The combination of these snapshots equals YOUR business.

Your business then becomes simple. The simplicity becomes visual as well as easily manageable. And this is how it works.

- *Simple enough?*
- *Think YOUR business is there?*
- *Want to take the test?*
- *Do you know what the test is?*

Read on and the answers become clear, as mud, maybe, yet that is why you are looking for entremaneur, to return to the simplicity that your business desires, demands, and needs.

The test is very simple—oh no, not yet, you must continue reading!

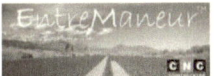

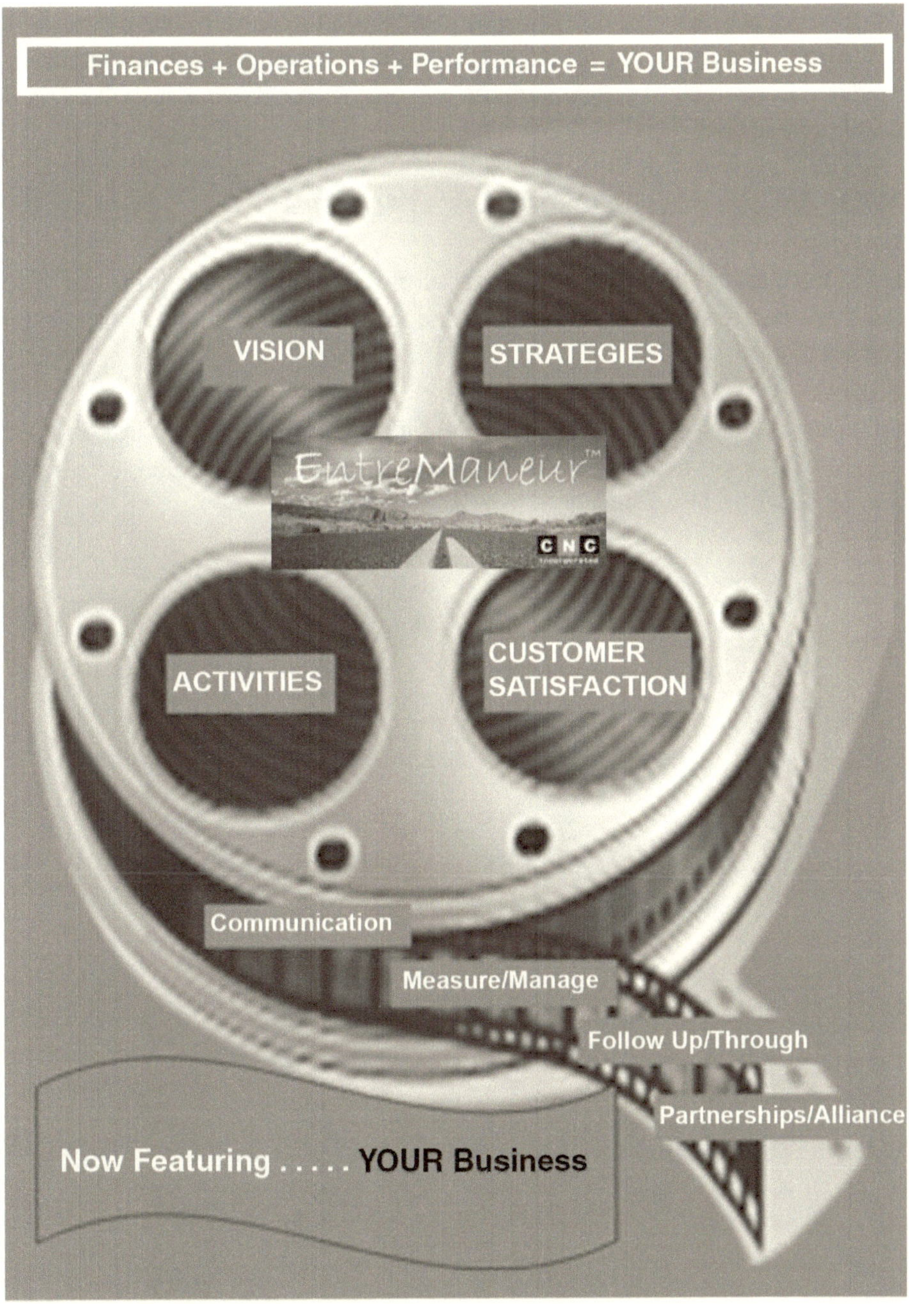
Finances + Operations + Performance = YOUR Business
VISION
STRATEGIES
EntreManeur™
ACTIVITIES
CUSTOMER SATISFACTION
Communication
Measure/Manage
Follow Up/Through
Partnerships/Alliance
Now Featuring . . . . . YOUR Business

The film reel represents continuous capturing of events that happen throughout business. Like in the world of digital photography, pictures "say a thousand words"—as the old saying goes—and most importantly, they provide realistic snapshots of current processes of the current situation and can easily be modified to characterize and to represent current processes/snapshots. This is entremaneur.

What Are the Actions and/or Costs (Activities)?

Let's start taking and developing pictures. The film reel represents your business, and each section becomes a snapshot that represents the process of entremaneur.

So entremaneur is simple. Still not buying it? Let's see if this will further assist in the "KISS"—an explanation, a visual and realistic view at vision, strategies, and activities and their simplicity in YOUR business!

Chapter 2

The Questionnaire

Questionnaire

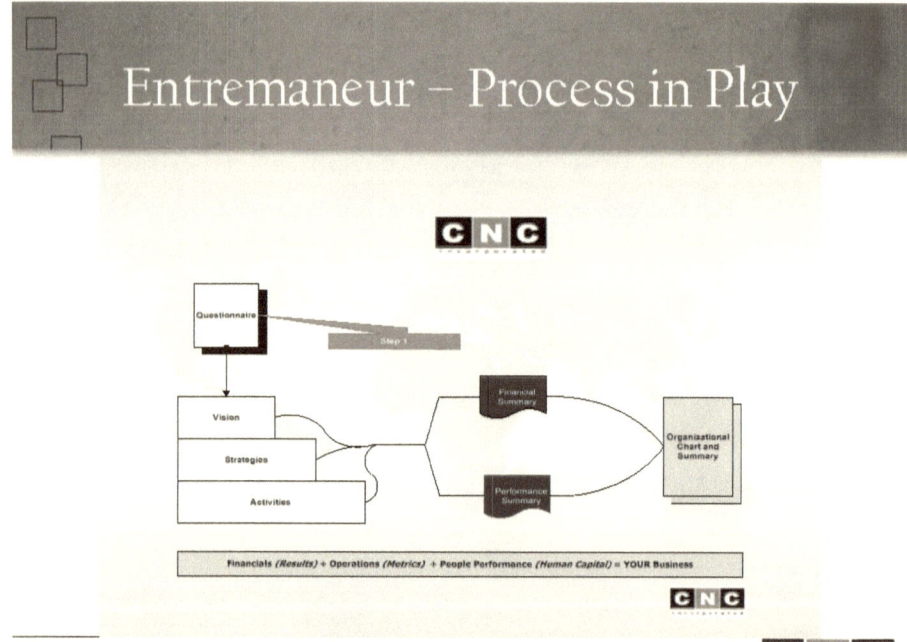

discover • plan • succeed

What Is It (Vision)?

Review your current business plan, create a business plan, assess against plans—simply—(snapshots) in real time. Change to meet or suit your needs (real time, redesign, forecast, what ifs, etc). The questionnaire is the simple approach to assessing YOUR business simplicity. Again, it may appear difficult at times, yet as the old expression goes, "no pain, no gain." You must review your current data points and use those to have a realistic starting point. Even if you don't have a clearly defined vision or strategies, this is the time to articulate these down into actionable and doable items that will create the measurement and management of YOUR business.

How Does It Work? What Will It Do for Me/Us (Strategies)?

Purpose and function of questionnaire:

- The questionnaire needs to provoke answers that will build the result, which is an organizational snapshot: summary financial *(results)* + operations *(metrics)* + people performance *(human capital)* = your business.
- The questions are designed to be simple—go figure—which are done in drop-down menus and pick and choose or free-flowing text.
- In certain areas, the drop-down menus will have the ability for multiselection (such as activities, etc.). And as in most scenarios similar to this, simply holding the control (Ctrl) and moving the mouse over and highlighting the items to be included will provide the result for that scenario/section.
- Inputs are of YOUR business, and in many cases they are confidential information about the finances, operations, and people of YOUR business. You will be logged into a secure site that will allow you only access to this information based upon secure log-in and password and licensed to you for a designated period.
- The results are simple and realistic information about YOUR business that you have provided, and this creates the snapshot of entremaneur.
- Each section is visual, shown as you will see it from the get-go and through-to completion, again keeping with the simplicity of strategically managing your business. The sections will provide a what, a purpose, and a how of each section, from samples to your actual information for immediate viewing.
- The outcomes are not traditional, yet simple. They are snapshots of YOUR business, literally and figuratively. The overall outcome or summary of the entire process—the entremaneur—is an organization chart, summary financial information, summary statistical information, summary performance information, all contained in a visual of the organization as if looking at a "house" and levels of that house as well as simple foundations—the statistical, financial, and performance information.

What Are the Actions and/or Costs (Activities)?

How to begin the process:

- ❑ Receive a demo of the process.
- ❑ Purchase the initial licensing agreement—minimum of six months.
- ❑ Log in to *www.cncincsolutions.com.*
- ❑ Create a log-in and password.
- ❑ Decide upon the level of detail you want to provide to determine the cost: high level (C suite), division level, department level.
- ❑ Complete the questionnaire: snapshots (*financial results),* operations *(metrics),* performance *(human capital).*
- ❑ Receive your "snapshot" of your organization—organizational chart, org summary, vision, strategies, activities, summary financial information, summary statistical information, summary performance information.
- ❑ Over the course of the licensing agreement, manipulate data to present proposed organization, projections; manage and measure current data in simple information; drill down into detail—financial, operations, and people performance summaries.
- ❑ Determine your next steps:
  - ○ Consultative approach—licensing agreement, live consulting, support, online support
  - ○ Continued online approach—licensing only and online support
- ❑ Entremaneur YOUR business with snapshots simply!

Chapter 3

Outcomes

Outcomes:

out·come *(out'kŭm')*
n.
An result; a consequence. See Synonyms at effect.

The results! You said and defined that you would do what by when. A visual that is agreed upon and consistent with all so that there are no misunderstandings exist with regards to what will be accomplished and measured and managed against. The completed film reel that depicts that *"Organizational Summary—Chart and Facts"* visually!

To start, you needed to see, feel, touch, and understand the flow and the importance of these sensory abilities—vision, strategies, activities, and outcomes. The starting point to all this is the completion of a simple task—although may seem complicated and time consuming/difficult at times, yet what is not time consuming in the beginning—in order to get to the result, which is business simplicity and snapshots that are in real time and can be changed with a few clicks to see new results, projections, proposals, etc.

So a few keyboard clicks away is YOUR business snapshots in real time—simple!

The development of the entremaneur process begins with the input of the company's specific data to create the initial snapshots—in other words, a questionnaire that guides the entremaneur flow.

This questionnaire can either be viewed as necessary or unnecessary. Obviously, you make the decision. Yes, there is upfront work that needs to take place to create simplicity and snapshots. As the old saying goes, "if you do what you have always done, you will get what you have always gotten." This is not necessarily a bad thing, yet if you are making money and/or are profitable at what expense? Do you know? Can you see in a "snapshot" where your money is being spent, where the activities are being done? Are they being done in the right place and by the right people and at the right amount of time? Are the people accomplishing your vision and strategies of the business, or has the vision and strategies become a writing exercise that went nowhere but into a lot of expensive screen savers, marketing materials, and not into the actual process or snapshots of the business?

If your answers are, "I don't know," then continue. If your answers are, "I don't really care," then stop!

Outcomes

What Is It (Vision)?

The outcomes, as viewed by the pictorial representation, are the overall entremaneur process. It is the visual of the organizational summary—chart and summary information pertaining to Financials *(Results)* + Operations *(Metrics)* + People Performance *(Human Capital)*.

How Does It Work? What Will It Do for Me/Us (Strategies)?

These items, culminated, form the snapshot of YOUR business outcomes and assist you in a real-time fashion to drive the *Financials (Results) + Operations Metrics) + People Performance (Human Capital)*.

- Visual Flow
  - Vision
  - Strategies
  - Activities
  - Organizational Structure with Overall Summary
  Financials(Results) + Operations (Metrics) + People Performance (Human Capital)of YOUR Business
  - Financial Summary *(Results)*
  - Operations Summary *(Metrics)*
    - Division/Departmental Breakdown of the Business—Summarized
    - Vision, Strategies and Activities Alignment Summary
  - People Performance Summary *(Human Capital)*
    - Performance Management—Activities by Position

What Are the Actions and/or Costs (Activities)?

Your job, if you choose to accept it—and no this will not self-destruct in five seconds, although now that is a concept—is to enter into agreeing to make your job easier and keeping your business simply ongoing. Complete the initial Entremaneur Questionnaire, and the rest is as they say—simple!

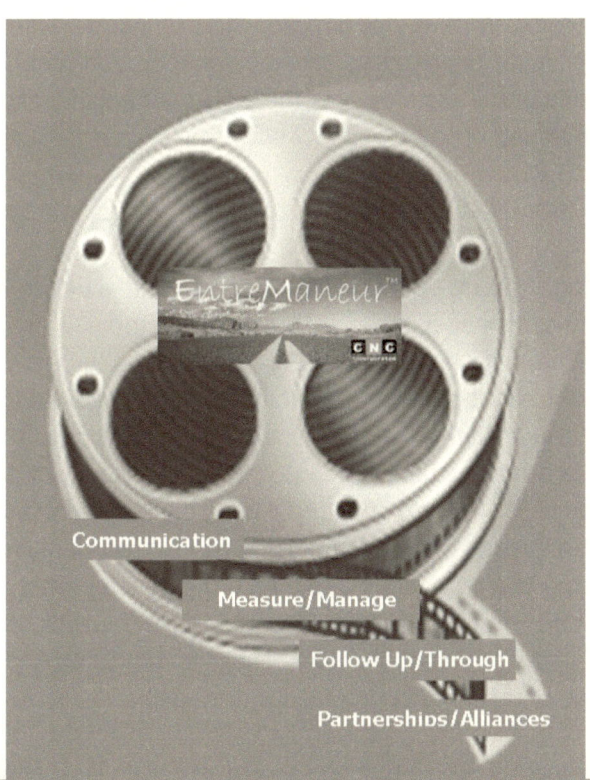

Organizational Chart and Summary: The Overview Snapshot of the Entremaneur Process

What Is It (Vision)?

How your business is organized and structured makes a major difference in working toward achieving results. The structure will drive the strategies and thus the performance. Whoever is directing the business must be synced with the vision and overall strategies. Without this direction, you cannot manage Performance *(human capital)*, create *(metrics)* Operations, and report on consistent *(results)* Financials. Your structure dictates how the vision, strategies, and subsequent activities will be carried out.

How Does It Work? What Will It Do for Me/Us (Strategies)?

It works by taking the data points, vision, strategy, and activities and inputting them into the questionnaire, along with simple information on finances and performance, people and general business, and generating summary snapshots of YOUR business. Some of them are more detailed and are considered the drill-down information that can be viewed in more detail, like taking a picture and zooming the lens to be sure that you are getting exactly the amount of detail you are seeking. This comes in the form of financial and people performance details. As for the snapshot summary, this is a form of one-page snapshot that pulls together the summary detail of all this information. An organizational chart, financial and performance details—company wide or departmental—depends upon your view (i.e., over—and under-stretched management time, burdened and unburdened costs, percentage of time and costs on activities—highest to lowest, etc.).

We believe the overall question that you should be asking is what won't it do for me or the company? What am I missing or missing out on if I don't take hold of my business in a snapshot and realistic viewpoint.

What Are the Actions and/or Costs (Activities)?

So what do you do now? Take control and complete the questionnaire to derive at the most important part of your business: the development of a strategic snapshot of all aspects—Financials *(results)* + Operations *(metrics)* + People Performance *(human capital)*—of YOUR business.

The costs have to be turned back to you. Is the investment of seeing your business in snapshot form and realistically and regularly changing the look and feel in a few clicks important to you? If you answer yes or even maybe, then the investment is complete, and you should move forward and begin snapping pictures! If the answer is no or unsure, then only you can decide and continue sitting on the sidelines and taking care of business as you always have and continue getting the same results and taking the same amount of time to get there, make changes, be aware that changes need to be made, identifying that the strategies are indeed being enforced and that the vision is clearly aligned to the strategies and what is being done as well as the performance of the people conducting the tasks are being aligned to the vision and strategies.

Outcome	Process Summary
Snapshot Process—Film Reel 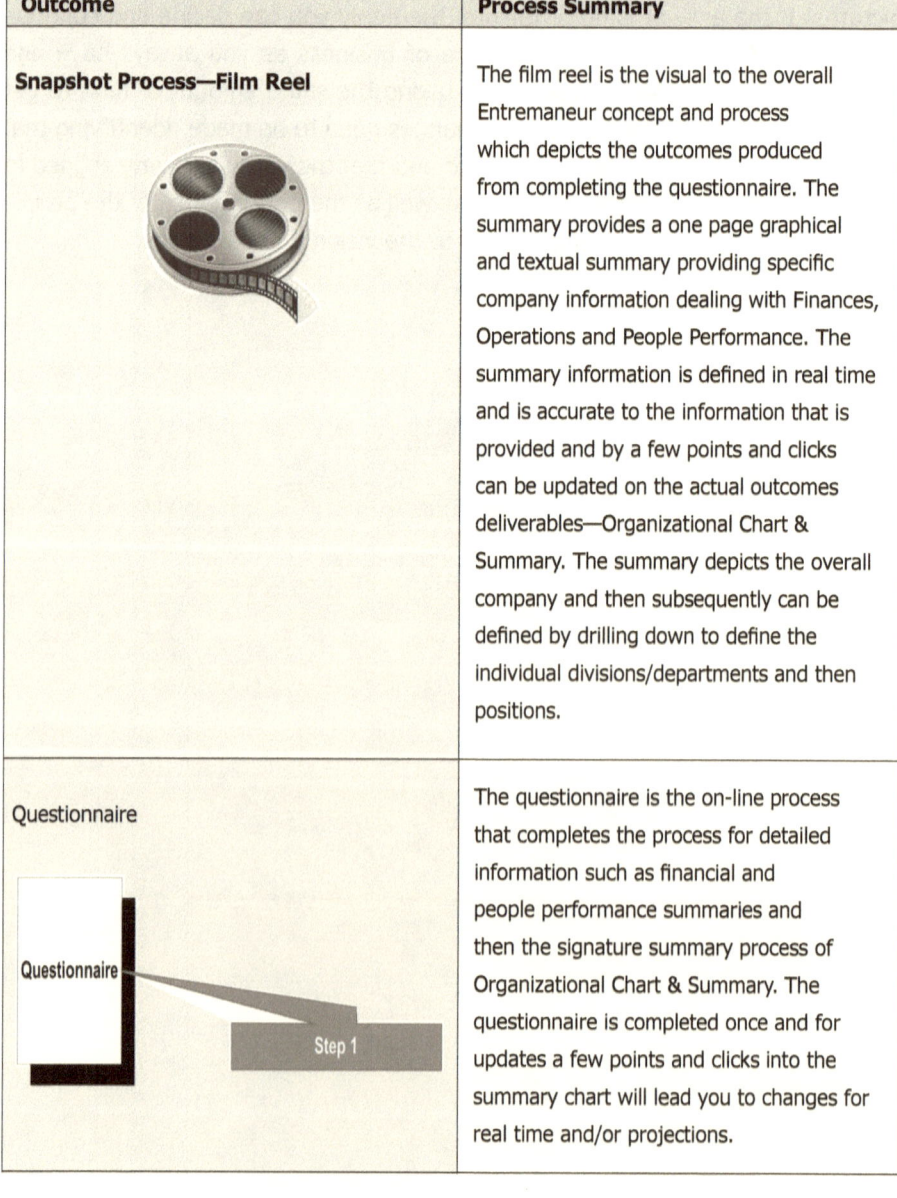	The film reel is the visual to the overall Entremaneur concept and process which depicts the outcomes produced from completing the questionnaire. The summary provides a one page graphical and textual summary providing specific company information dealing with Finances, Operations and People Performance. The summary information is defined in real time and is accurate to the information that is provided and by a few points and clicks can be updated on the actual outcomes deliverables—Organizational Chart & Summary. The summary depicts the overall company and then subsequently can be defined by drilling down to define the individual divisions/departments and then positions.
Questionnaire	The questionnaire is the on-line process that completes the process for detailed information such as financial and people performance summaries and then the signature summary process of Organizational Chart & Summary. The questionnaire is completed once and for updates a few points and clicks into the summary chart will lead you to changes for real time and/or projections.

Outcome	Process Summary
Financial Summary 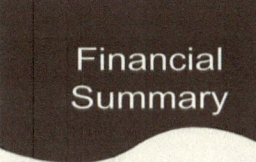	The financial summary is the detailed information based upon the company and data inputted from the questionnaire. The information here drills down to the detail of the company, division/department and position(s). This information is a mini budget and is not meant to replace a budgeting process, yet augment it and provide detail and summary information when drilling down into the company, division/department and position(s) as well as summary information when incorporated into the Organizational Chart & Summary.
Performance Summary 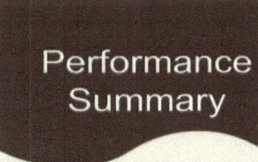	In this format you are provided with the people performance summary detailing out activities, times, dollars, etc. that formulate the position and the tasks that are accomplished to meet the defined organizational strategies. These activities are mapped against the defined organizational strategies in summary and drill down detail. The summary data is in the Organizational Chart and Summary and the detail is contained here within the Performance Summary. This information provides summary and details pertaining to performance management and like the Financial Summary is not meant to replace company performance management systems, yet augment the current process and provide real time summary information on tasks, activities, %, dollars and the likes of what is happening and where.

Outcome	Process Summary
Organizational Chart & Summary— **ENTREMANEUR** 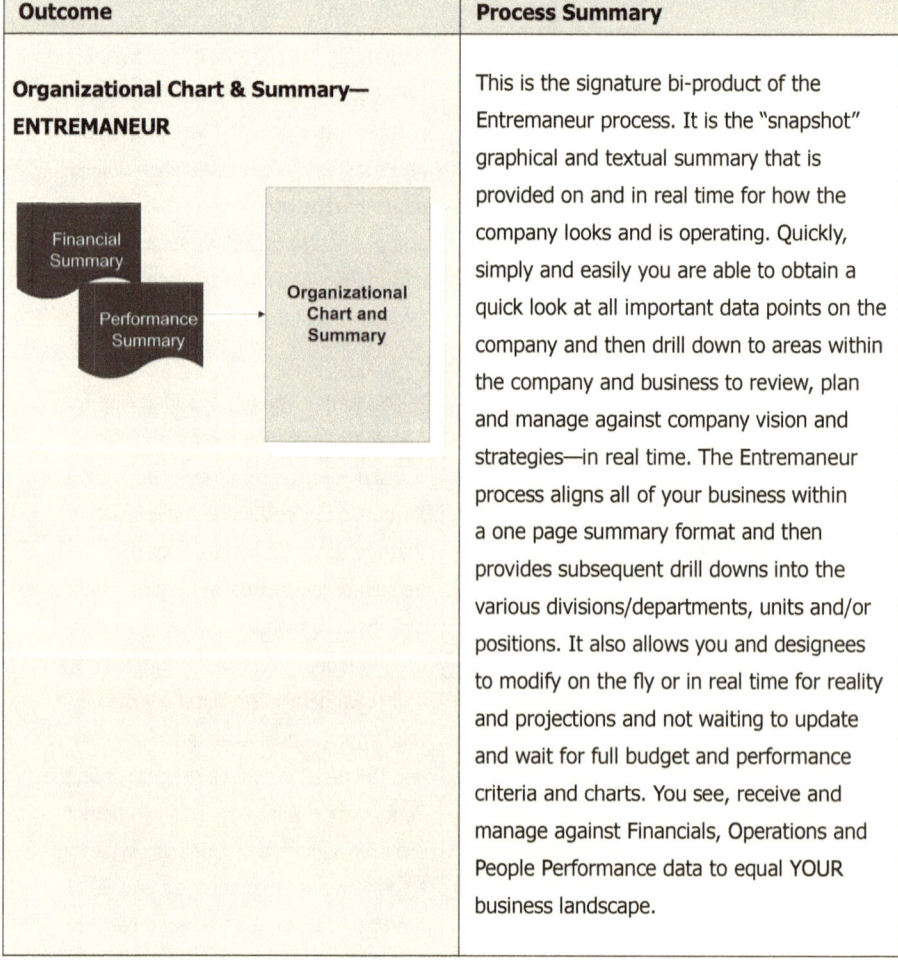	This is the signature bi-product of the Entremaneur process. It is the "snapshot" graphical and textual summary that is provided on and in real time for how the company looks and is operating. Quickly, simply and easily you are able to obtain a quick look at all important data points on the company and then drill down to areas within the company and business to review, plan and manage against company vision and strategies—in real time. The Entremaneur process aligns all of your business within a one page summary format and then provides subsequent drill downs into the various divisions/departments, units and/or positions. It also allows you and designees to modify on the fly or in real time for reality and projections and not waiting to update and wait for full budget and performance criteria and charts. You see, receive and manage against Financials, Operations and People Performance data to equal YOUR business landscape.

<table>
<tr><td colspan="42" rowspan="2">Organizational Chart & Summary
Finances + Operations + People Performance
"Company X"</td><td colspan="5">Summary by Level</td></tr>
<tr><td>B$</td><td>UB$</td><td>H$A</td><td>L$A</td><td>Hdct</td></tr>
<tr><td colspan="42">Business Leader Level/CEO</td><td></td><td></td><td></td><td></td><td></td></tr>
<tr><td colspan="6">Business Unit (BU)/ Dept Level</td><td colspan="6">Business Unit (BU)/ Dept Level</td><td colspan="6">Business Unit (BU)/ Dept Level</td><td colspan="6">Business Unit (BU)/ Dept Level</td><td colspan="6">Business Unit (BU)/ Dept Level</td><td colspan="6">Business Unit (BU)/ Dept Level</td><td colspan="6">Business Unit (BU/ Dept Level</td><td></td><td></td><td></td><td></td><td></td></tr>
<tr><td colspan="3">Next Level BU</td><td colspan="3">Next Level BU</td><td colspan="3">Next Level BU</td><td colspan="3">Next Level BU</td><td colspan="3">Next Level BU</td><td colspan="3">Next Level BU</td><td colspan="3">Next Level BU</td><td colspan="3">Next Level BU</td><td colspan="3">Next Level BU</td><td colspan="3">Next Level BU</td><td colspan="3">Next Level BU</td><td colspan="3">Next Level BU</td><td colspan="3">Next Level BU</td><td colspan="3">Next Level BU</td><td></td><td></td><td></td><td></td><td></td></tr>
<tr><td colspan="2">Indiv. Level</td><td colspan="2">Indiv. Level</td><td colspan="2">Indiv. Level</td><td colspan="2">Indiv. Level</td><td colspan="2">Indiv. Level</td><td colspan="2">Indiv. Level</td><td colspan="2">Indiv. Level</td><td colspan="2">Indiv. Level</td><td colspan="2">Indiv. Level</td><td colspan="2">Indiv. Level</td><td colspan="2">Indiv. Level</td><td colspan="2">Indiv. Level</td><td colspan="2">Indiv. Level</td><td colspan="2">Indiv. Level</td><td colspan="2">Indiv. Level</td><td colspan="2">Indiv. Level</td><td colspan="2">Indiv. Level</td><td colspan="2">Indiv. Level</td><td colspan="2">Indiv. Level</td><td colspan="2">Indiv. Level</td><td colspan="2">Indiv. Level</td><td></td><td></td><td></td><td></td><td></td></tr>
</table>

Totals					

B$ = *Burdened Dollars*
UB$ = *Unburdened Dollars*
H$A = *Highest Activity Dollars*
L$A = *Lowest Activity Dollars*
Hdct = *Total Headcount*

Company Specific Statistical Summary (Finances & Operations)

People and Time

Div/Dept	Budget Total ee's	Actual Total ee's	Budget Mgmt ee's	Actual Mgmt ee's	Budget Mgmt: Worker ratio	Actual Mgmt: Worker ratio	Budget 1/1 Mgmt Positions	Actual 1/1 Mgmt Positions	Budget Under Utilized Mgrs	Actual Under Utilized Mgrs	Budget Over Utilized Mgrs	Actual Over Utilized Mgrs	Budget Lowest Activity Time	Actual Lowest Activity Time	Budget Highest Activity Time	Actual Highest Activity Time
Div, Dept																

Drop down menu to see division, unit and department specific information that rolls up to the total below. Clicking on a specific row for one of the divisions, units and/or departments will link to specific drill down on the group (organizational chart, finances and operations (people and time and dollars) and people (activities).

Totals																

Dollars

Div/Dept	Budget Total all ee's Un-burdened	Actual Total all ee's Burdened	Budget Total ee's Un-burdened	Actual Total ee's Burdened	Budget Mgmt Un-burdened	Actual Mgmt Burdened	Budget Highest Activity	Actual Highest Activity	Budget Lowest Activity	Actual Lowest Activity	Budget Growth 1 Year	Actual Growth 1 Year	Budget Growth 2 Years	Actual Growth 2 Years	Budget Growth 3 Years	Actual Growth 3 Years
Div, Dept																

Drop down menu to see division, unit and department specific information that rolls up to the total below. Clicking on a specific row for one of the divisions, units and/or departments will link to specific drill down on the group (organizational chart, finances and operations (people and time and dollars) and people (activities).

Totals																

Vision, Strategy, Activity Alignment – Company & Division/Dept/Unit

Vision	Strategy	Division/Dept/Unit								
		Activities	Activities	Activities	Activities	Activities	Activities	Activities	Activities	Activities
Company mantra is the main vision statement that is the guiding principle for the entire organization – what it stands for|	Company Wide – alignment is based upon how primary activities for a group matches company wide Strategies. The norm is no more than 5 overall Company Strategies.									

This is for highest percentage and primary activities overall for the Division, Department and/or Unit. Activities will align to the company strategies based upon the overall alignment to meeting the specific strategies and will be primary to this result. Only primary and highest percentage of time activities will be accounted for in this area, therefore not all activities will necessarily be listed. Any activities that are not primary and yet come up with an overall high percentage of time affiliated with them will be accounted for. This will be highlighted as a potential opportunity for further clarification and reclassification or alignment within the right area of expertise, etc.

Chapter 4

Vision

Vision:

*"**Vision**—A guiding theme that articulates the nature of the business/library and its intentions for the future, based upon how management believes the environment will unfold. A **vision** is informed, share, competitive and enabling." (http://en.mimi.hu/marketingweb/vision.html)*

The vision refers to the way in which the organization sees itself. What and why we are here and what does that look like. A vision clearly articulates a broad snapshot of the company. The vision must then be communicated properly and consistently, and it is everyone's responsibility to understand and explain it.

A simple statement not something that is verbose, yet something short, succinct, and actionable that will withstand time of YOUR business.

Vision leads to strategies. The strategies are the defining points of the company's vision and guides to achieving the vision.

Vision

What Is It (Vision)?

Can you see everything that everyone is doing in your company? Can you see every activity and how it is performed by every individual? Are you a mind reader, and/or do you expect your people to be mind readers? Everything about who and what your business is and what it does must start with a vision and subsequent strategies to make the vision possible.

Most of you read this and begin to think "mumbo jumbo, jargon, touchy feely," etc. Yet when you stop for five minutes and add up the hourly rate of each individual, starting at your direct-report level and the time and other resources for misunderstanding, miscommunication, errors, rework, fragmentation, duplication, off task—the list goes on, the figure is staggering.

Do not go away and have a vision and strategy session if you do not plan to use them consistently and constantly throughout running your business. Otherwise, you will get what you have always gotten, which is a repeat of the above—errors rework, etc.

DO NOT MAKE WRITING A VISION A FUTILITY IN WRITING, SIGNING, AND POSTING ACTIVITY THAT GOES NOWHERE, INCLUDING NOT IN PEOPLE'S MINDS!

Do make it real. Once you write your vision clearly and have it articulated simply, it does not need to be something and should not be something that is redone year to year. Your vision is a simple statement that reflects the overall essence of your business.

Entremaneur's vision is—

Entremaneur is a process . . . clear, simple, and concise—a way to measure, monitor, and manage your business and create simplicity for real-time use of **Finances *(results)* + Operations *(metrics)* + People Performance *(human capital)*!**

How Does It Work? What Will It Do for Me/Us (Strategies)?

The strategies begin to define how you will make the vision real. The strategies should be done, looked at, and redefined on a year-to-year basis, as business conditions, accomplishments, etc., change, and therefore the approach to making the vision real changes.

The vision should become your basic company mantra. Yes, your initial who we are and what we do, the beginning of the thirty-second elevator spiel, your initial marketing of the company. That is why it is so important to be clear, simple, short, and articulated throughout, so everyone understands and can say it, feel it, speak it, and present it—an initial sound bite of your business.

This is why you do not go away year after year to write a vision—your company vision should remain constant. The understanding and articulation of such makes it real.

Are we supporting "stepford" methodology? In the beginning yes, again unless you are "bewitched" and twinkle your nose so everyone gets it one time. At the same time, it is highly important to be sure that your vision is your guiding mantra—sound bite example, marketing of your company, one statement, simple, easy and understood.

What Are the Actions and/or Costs (Activities)?

You *MUST* begin with your direct reports, without assumptions and bias. Every one of them *must* get it, see it, and feel it, as they are your decipals, taking and managing it to and in the business.

Vision leads to strategies. The strategies are the defining points of the company's vision, and guides to achieving the vision.

Chapter 5

Strategy

Strategies:

"strat·e·gy (străt'ə-jē)
n., pl.—*gies*.

- *The science and art of using all the forces of a nation to execute approved plans as effectively as possible during peace or war.*
- *The science and art of military command as applied to the overall planning and conduct of large-scale combat operations.*
- *A plan of action resulting from strategy or intended to accomplish a specific goal. See synonyms at plan.*
- *The art or skill of using stratagems in endeavors such as politics and business.*
- *[French stratégie, from Greek stratēgiā, office of a general, from stratēgos, general. See stratagem.]*

The strategies are the actual how-tos for accomplishing what the vision outlines. This is broken down by the corporate and each operating unit/department within the organization. They are actionable items that can be implemented and drilled down into activities—the individual's tasks of achievable results. So the simplicity is about being able to have everyone in the company only three levels from the overall vision at any time.

Strategies take us to the specifics—the activities. They define the overall value of what the company will be working toward to achieve the vision, and subsequently the next layer is the specific tasks or activities that will be accomplished via divisions, departments, units, and/or positions.

Strategy

What Is It (Vision)?

Strategy is truly the full identification of YOUR vision. The strategies that are depicted or derived from your business vision will guide the vision and then set the stage for preparing the people performance (human capital) tasks to be completed. Your strategies will more than likely change from year to year, which is usually the planning time. The vision will or should not change; yet based upon accomplishments from previous years or quarters, your strategies will likely change.

How Does It Work? What Will It Do for Me/Us (Strategies)?

Again keeping with the theme—can you guess? yes, you are right, simplicity—you input your organizational strategies based upon the questionnaire. There are samples for you to view and identify how yours should be articulated. The general rule of thumb is to keep the strategies as statements and short. There should be approximately five to seven overall business strategies. The reason for this is that your individual's activities or tasks will define these further. Again, you do not want to complicate this or overassess this process. The tasks do this for you, and too, simple and concise, are derived from drop-down menus for simplicity. Your strategies can be free-flowing or can be derived from a listing of basic categories. The more you put in, the more it becomes YOUR company and not a generic process.

What Are the Actions and/or Costs (Activities)?

The actions—what do you think?—complete the questionnaire. Yes, simple! A broken record sounds like this: if you continue to do what you have done, you will continue to get what you have gotten, and at what expense? It is your choice. Don't stand alone. Get entremaneured!

Strategies take us to the specifics—the activities. They define the overall value of what the company will be working toward to achieve the vision, and subsequently the next layer is the specific tasks or activities that will be accomplished via divisions, departments, units, and/or positions.

Chapter 6

Activities

Activities:

ac·tiv·i·ty *(ăk-tĭv'ĭ-tē)*
n. pl. ***ac·tiv·i·ties***

1. The state of being active.
2. Energetic action or movement; liveliness.
   a. A specified pursuit in which a person partakes.
   b. An educational process or procedure intended to stimulate learning through actual experience.
3. The intensity of a radioactive source.
4. The ability to take part in a chemical reaction.
5. A physiological process: respiratory activity.

The activities are the actual *tasks* that are accomplished and are matched to the job profiles and competencies (depending upon how your organization defines this) of the position accomplishing the task. This then becomes the "what is that I do and I what I do fits into the organization" sound track. Everyone in the organization should be no more than three levels away from the overall vision of the company—simple and easy! The specific to-dos in order to accomplish strategies, which are accomplishing/meeting the company's vision!

So you see the simplicity? The vision, strategies, and activities are the layers that create the information you will use to create your entremaneur of YOUR business and use to measure and manage regularly in simple snapshots! These are then seen as the outcomes that will become your strategic snapshots and mantra on going.

Activities

What Is It (Vision)?

Activities are just that. What we defined earlier are the actual tasks that are completed to meet the defined business strategies and the defined vision. Activities are broken down by task categories and are picked and defined in 5 percent increments to equal 100 percent of an individual's time. This assists in defining the Overview—Organizational Summary—Chart and Summary.

How Does It Work? What Will It Do for Me/Us (Strategies)?

Again, keeping with simplicity or KISS (keep it simple, stupid), completing the initial questionnaire is the process for getting to this point. You choose the positions as an overall in the department or company, or break it down individually and then cross-reference a list of tasks from a drop-down menu and simply assign a percentage to those tasks. The percentages are in 5 percent increments and can only equal 100 percent per position or grouping. Yes, we know that everyone does more than 100 percent, yet we must be realistic in order to have realistic snapshot results!

What Are the Actions and/or Costs (Activities)?

Choose a course of action, such as completing the questionnaire, which will entail gathering the appropriate information—financial and performance mainly—so that you can accurately input the data. Your time is the cost. Not completing it is the cost. Completing it becomes the start of the savings and simplicity. Once you have done the "painstaking" job of gathering the appropriate information and completing the questionnaire, which is intuitive and driven via on-line formatting, then you have completed the toughest task; and it is a matter of updating, changing, modifying, etc., by mere clicks of the keys—of course, once you have logged into your secure information!

So you see the simplicity? The vision, strategies, and activities are the layers that create the information you will use to create your entremaneur of YOUR business and use to measure and manage regularly in simple snapshots! These are then seen as the outcomes that will become your strategic snapshots and mantra on going.

Chapter 7

Where's the Simplicity?

Simplicity?

Where's the Simplicity?

What Is It (Vision)?

KISS. Do you remember this from school? I do, as it was drilled into me over and over. I cannot say that I always followed it, yet I remembered so much it was always in my mind, and I constantly strived to move back to simplicity. Simply put:

K = Keep I = It S = Simple S = Stupid

The process is simple. We complicate it. Keeping it simple should be simple—therefore, entremaneur! Don't think of it as or make it a process yet a part of doing business regularly. Clearly seeing, identifying, working with, changing and modifying "things" simply!

How Does It Work? What Will It Do for Me/Us (Strategies)?

What you just followed and processed are immediately transferable to your business. Here's how:

- The results are based upon what you input.
- The outcomes are the realistic (your data) entremaneur process snapshots.
  - Once entered, all you have to do is update—as simple as a click or two away.
  - The Pain Points: Doing it the first time. Establishing the baseline. Without a baseline, you have nothing to manage your business process from or toward. If you do what you have always done, then you will get what you have always gotten. Not always bad, yet at what expense, literally and figuratively?
  - The Simplicity: Updating is easy and regular. Again, a click or two will modify the entire process and outcomes to view in real time actuals and what-ifs.

You have the information. Place it in one simple location. Develop it upfront. Put it into daily play (Vision—Strategies—Activities). Make it real. Keep it simple. And above, all use it daily. It is your on-going, real-time business mantra—it is entremaneur!

What Are the Actions and/or Costs (Activities)?

The actions are, as Nike says, "Just Do It"! Continue doing what you have been doing, and you will continue to get the same results. If the results appear to be working and profitable, then ask, at what expense, what am I leaving on the table? If you say you are happy with where you are and don't care about making or keeping things simple, ahead of the competition, on top of your game, or whatever other expression comes to mind or is "in" now, then stop here. If you are interested in continuing to understand how to simply measure and manage YOUR ongoing business and with the ease of simplicity, change, and the likes from literally seeing and using snapshots, then continue! ***Simple enough?***

The Test: You have been patient from chapter 1!

So now I guess I can you tell you what the test is—ready, set . . . ah no . . . you have to call us. After all, we are a consulting firm! Okay, okay, the test is SIMPLE and is gratuitous! Yes, that is right—FREE!

Give us one hour and we will give you the diagnosis, and then you decide whether to entremaneur or not! See simply! Can you afford an hour?

The Other "—maneur"

Chapter 8

Strategic Alliances/Partnerships

Strategic Alliances/Partnerships

What Is It (Vision)?

Strategic alliances and partnerships are a part of our business whether they are internal or external. They are the individuals and/or groups that provide bridges to the business in a variety of fashions, whether they are stakeholders, consulting groups, attorneys, vendors, accountants, task forces, etc. These groups or individuals are the *what* in the equation of the business at large.

How Does It Work? What Will It Do for Me/Us (Strategies)?

Usually strategic alliances/partners provide the guidance to the business that is objective and fits well into the strategic plan. They are the ones that play devils advocate to what is working, not working, planned, unplanned, if you do this or don't do this, this is what you will get or not get. It provides YOUR business with trusted internal or external advisors that will assist in guiding the business and in the end the entremaneurial process—snapshots of your current state, proposed state, and future state. In other words, they keep you honest and "your film on the reel" so that everyone is working toward Vision, Strategies, and Activities, and that all see there are only three steps from the company's vision at any one time and how they fit to the business. Your best asset is your people, so capitalize on their knowledge and keeping them happy, interested, supportive, and communicative! Entremaneur them!

What Are the Actions and/or Costs (Activities)?

The actions are to be sure that you have the right advocates in your business or associated with your business, whether internal or external. This like any other part of running the business; it is a process and can be ever changing depending, upon the strategies and subsequent activities that you define. Always, always, always establish guidelines to measure, monitor, and manage these relationships and the roles and responsibilities, which clearly aligns to communicate, communicate, communicate, and, of course, entremaneur the business. The process of entremaneur creates the guides for these relationships and therefore creates the ease and simplicity on what they do, contribute, purpose, etc. Actions and costs for each business are different as each alliance-partner relationship is supported and utilized differently. Your goal is to understand this like you would the roles and responsibilities of your employees in general.

Chapter 9

Ownership

Ownership

What Is It (Vision)?

Wow! Ownership is truly the process of taking on responsibilities and owning the actions, decisions, results, and the measuring against the overall strategies and vision of the business consistently and constantly.

How Does It Work? What Will It Do for Me/Us (Strategies)?

Much like anything else, ownership is just that. How it works is how you establish this in your business. What accountability and criteria that you allow to perpetrate within and then holding individuals and groups accountable. Entremaneur is the setup guidelines and measuring and monitoring system for this ownership and accountability. Putting the information in an easily entered, read, understood, and useable format provides the guide for your business. Making it difficult makes it difficult to implement which makes it difficult to measure and manage and therefore makes it complex. If this is the concept and approach that you want, then join the club. You are not alone, as most businesses are in the same boat. We tend to shift toward complexity and less toward simplicity. Entremaneurize yourself now and simplify your life!

What Are the Actions and/or Costs (Activities)?

The actions are to align individual's roles and responsibilities to the business and the processes. Understanding what they do, where they spend their time, and subsequently what activities they are doing will assist in defining the actions. Establishing the process is the hard part and the easy part. Okay, in layman's terms: starting the process and inputting the initial information is the hard part; using it, adjusting it, etc., is the easy part—that is the entremaneurial way.

Chapter 10

Communication

What's the "Talk" on Communication?

What Is It (Vision)?

Communicate

Communicate

Communicate

One of the biggest things that is accessible to us all and yet the one thing that is most assumed and misused.

Keeping with the theme of simplicity the entremaneur way, these following steps should and could guide you to communicate or to learn to communicate in the entremaneur fashion—simply.

Set the vision, explain the vision, and use the vision as your company's "sound bit/mantra."

Set and implement the strategies to achieve the vision, align the strategies against the business leaders, align against business/units/departments, and align the strategies to the individual positions.

How Does It Work? What Will It Do for Me/Us (Strategies)?

You, as the business, must encourage communication as well as be the implementer and set the example for all to follow. Without a guide, how do people know what they are supposed to do and how to process? Communication is the biggest thing we have going for or against us. It truly does not matter what processes we implement and does not matter how good our intentions are, if we don't have open communications that are consistent and constant, then the processes will tend to be just that—processes! It then becomes like a reel of film where the film gets stuck or caught up on the reel itself—a mess!

Create entremaneur because you want simplicity. Create entremaneur because you care about your business and want to look at your current state and be able to modify on the fly to understand what the future state would look like with the click of a button. Sound simple? IT IS!

What Are the Actions and/or Costs (Activities)?

Monitor, measure, manage:

Financials *(results)* + Operations *(metrics)* + People Performance *(human capital)*

=

Visions and Strategies

=

Communications

=

Entremaneur

=

YOUR Business!

If you don't get it, then your team (management, professional, worker, and the like) will not get it. Simply put, it will result in rework, miscommunication, errors, fragmentation, wasted dollars, over—and underused management time, etc. Even if YOUR business is making dollars in spite of you and them, the waste is enormous, and the question needs to be asked: at what expense? Making money is great and wonderful, yet if you are wasting equally as much in poor practices and management of resources at large, then what are you really making?

Who complicates communication? We do! Who uncomplicates it or at least gets it to a two-way flow of information? We do! Information gathered and presented from entremaneur will give the guide necessary to communicate to and from!

Again, the reiteration that is necessary here is that the CEO defines and directs this. So where most CEOs are focused on the sales, improving the operations and profitability, they lose sight of the most SIMPLE and important aspect—and that is communication. Entremaneur brings back the simplicity to business and allows the company to get and stay on track with a SIMPLE snapshot and overlay to the business of Finances + Operations + People Performance ongoing and real time that you have no excuse not to communicate, nor does your team!

So Entremaneur now or continue doing the same things you have been doing, and you continue to get the same things you have always gotten!

Appendix

What's Next?

Like anything else in life, this book does not suggest or provide all the answers, especially to fit everyone's needs, tastes, desires, wants, etc. What it does is hopefully provide you with a realistic look and concepts at how to do things a little differently, to get results that are more palatable. You make the difference on how to approach and implement solutions that are simple and easy to use, or complex and cumbersome. Hopefully, your choice is the first—simple and easy. What you have learned here is that this approach is constant, and not every decision that you make is always going to be the right one, or the only one. Most times, as you get into something, you will adjust, measure, and monitor and make changes as necessary, yet make it easy, simple, and most of all fun.

This is a series of helpful hints on keeping business simplistic and fun, and how the two can and should work together. As you continue to implement opportunities facilitated within, you too will learn the simplicity that can come from all that is within the world that you work—business!

If you cannot measure it, then what are you managing against?

If you are measuring, what were the measurements created from, and what are they being managed against?

If you cannot clearly answer these questions, then you do not clearly have a vision and strategies that are outlined and understood throughout the business.

TRANSFER AND USE. STOP THE COMPLEXITY. MAKE IT SIMPLE!

Giving Thanks and Some . . .

I believe it is appropriate to give thanks and acknowledgment to those integral in making this happen. I also believe it needs to be appropriately placed and timed; otherwise, we have the Academy Awards acceptance speech in writing. (Get the cane and pull him off and say, "Thanks, we'll call you . . . NOT!) Anything lengthy here will take away from the lessons being presented; therefore, my thanks are as follows:

I would like to thank the Academy—kidding, just checking to make sure that everyone still has a sense of humor!

Actually, thanks to everyone, as this book is a result of each and every one of us, and the lessons learned come from all of us, then, now, and on going.

Thanks!

Entremaneur

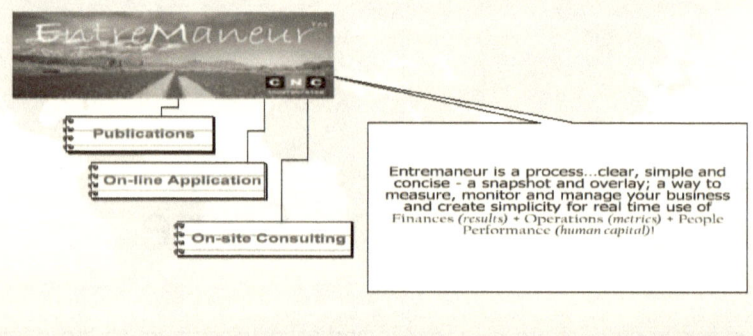

Entremaneur is a process...clear, simple and concise - a snapshot and overlay; a way to measure, monitor and manage your business and create simplicity for real time use of Finances *(results)* + Operations *(metrics)* + People Performance *(human capital)*!

discover • plan • succeed

www.ingramcontent.com/pod-product-compliance
Lightning Source LLC
Chambersburg PA
CBHW021904170526
45157CB00005B/1966